NOODLES

Published by: Cross Media Ltd.
13 Berners Street, London W1T 3LH, UK
Tel: 020-7436-1960   Fax: 020-7436-1930

Copyright of Photography and Text © Cross Media Ltd. 2001

Project Manager: Kazuhiro Marumo
Editor: J.L.Rollinson
Designer: Misa Watanabe
Photographer: Naomi Igawa, Hiroshi Mitani
Recipes: Nobuko Motohashi
Chef: Miyoko Yoshimura (Akasha Cooking School)
Coordinator: Masahiko Goto. Thanks to: Akasha Tōkōdō & Sono Aoki

ISBN 1-897701-87-X
Printed in Japan

All about noodles

A healthy source of protein and carbohydrate

Wheat is thought to be the first crop ever cultivated, and making noodles from wheat has been traced to the Hwang Ho region of China between the third and fifth centuries. Originally noodles were circular or oval, later developing into the long strings that are familiar today. Noodles were gradually adopted by various cultures around the world, each adapting them to their own cooking style. Noodles were introduced to Japan about 1,200 years ago. The main nutritional components of noodles are carbohydrate and protein. The carbohydrate converts to energy that is fairly long lasting, and the protein content is beneficial to both the circulatory system and to muscle, making noodles a healthy addition to the diet.

3

Different noodles and how to cook them

Subtle textures and tastes:

The main ingredient for any kind of noodle is wheat, and the taste and texture of noodles varies according to which type of wheat is used and in what proportion. For the *soba* noodle, the *Juwari* variety is made from 100% buckwheat flour, where as the *Nihachi soba* is 80% buckwheat flour and 20% plain flour. Cooking time also alters the texture of noodles, and the length of cooking time - for *udon* noodles in particular - varies to suit your preference, obviously a shorter cooking time produces a more *al dente* noodle. The different ingredients used in *ramen* dishes (Chinese egg noodle soup), such as soy sauce, *miso* (fermented soybean paste), or chillies, really changes the character of the basic *ramen* soup stock.

SOBA

Although these noodles are at their best when handmade and fresh, dried *soba* is also good and is obviously easy to keep. To cook the dried *soba*, boil it, lower the heat if bubbling over, and once cooked, drain, rinse, squeeze and turn it under cold running water.

UDON · · · · · · · · · · · · · · ·

Udon are made from wheat flour, which is kneaded with salt and water, and then flattened out. The thickness of these noodles varies, and this affects the cooking time. There is also a pre-boiled variety of *udon* that literally take a minute to cook.

SOMEN · · · · · · · · · · · · · · ·

These are also made from wheat flour and kneaded with salt and water. They are then stretched out into almost silk-like threads, and dried. Boil about 3 litres of water and cook the *somen* for $1\frac{1}{2}$ minutes. Straight after boiling, soak them in cold water, rinse, and squeeze them under running water.

RAMEN · · · · · · · · · · · · · · ·

Ramen are made from wheat flour and a special type of carbonated water, kneaded and stretched into a range of thicknesses, some are curled, some flattened, but the more common variety are thick and long. Boil them in plenty of water so that they don't stick together and stir occasionally.

How to make noodle soup

The secret of great noodle dishes is the soup stock:

Dashi is the basic Japanese soup stock

Dashi is made from dried kelp and bonito flakes, and is the equivalent of chicken stock in Western cooking. To make the soup for *soba* noodles, *udon* noodles, and *somen* noodles, extra seasoning is added to the soup stock.

Makes 1 litre
1 sheet of kelp (10cm × 10cm)
1.5 litres water
30g bonito flakes
50ml soy sauce
50ml *mirin*

1 Make a few slits in the kelp, and cook it in the water on a medium heat, removing the kelp just before it boils.

2 Add the bonito flakes to the pan, bring to a boil, and then strain.

3 Boil the *mirin* in another pan to remove the alcohol.

4 Add the *mirin* to the reduced soup stock (now approx. 700ml) and bring to the boil, add the soy sauce and bring it to the boil again.

For the cold soup:

This has to be more concentrated, use 400ml soup stock to 100ml soy sauce and 100ml *mirin*, and cool it in the fridge.

Chilled Soba with Dried Seaweed
● ざるそば *Zaru Soba* ●

Serves 1

100g *soba* noodles
¼ spring onion
1 *myoga* (optional)
some dried seaweed
some *wasabi*
150ml cold soup

* See page 4 how to cook noodles
* See page 7 how to make cold soup

1 Chop up the spring onion 2mm width. Slice up the *myoga* 2mm width, soak it in water and then drain it.

2  Transfer the *soba* to cold water immediately after cooking, squeeze it gently, and then drain it. Arrange the *soba* on a serving plate, and sprinkle with the dried seaweed (cut into fine strips).

3 Serve the cold soup in a deep bowl. Arrange the spring onion, *myoga*, and *wasabi* on a small plate, so that people can add the condiment they like to their own cold soup before eating.

Soba Noodles with Tempura

天ぷらそば *Tempura Soba*

This dish is great for spoiling yourself, and is equally a hit if you are having people over for dinner.

* See page 4 how to cook noodles
* See page 6 how to make noodle soup

Serves 1

100g *soba* noodles
350ml noodle soup
2 shrimps
50g spinach
¼ spring onion
some *shichimi*
(optional)

1 Shell the shrimps, cut off only the tips of the tails, devein, and make a few cuts on the undersides.

[for the batter]

½ egg

50g plain flour, sifted

80ml cold water

some vegetable
or sunflower oil

2 To make the batter, beat the egg and lightly mix with the cold water and flour.

3 Heat the oil in a heavy-based deep pan.

4 Dip the shrimps in the batter, and deep-fry until they float on the surface of the oil. Once cooked, place them on kitchen paper to remove excess oil.

Tip!

To keep the batter 'light' for frying, don't over mix it.

5 Cook the spinach, drain it and cut it into 5cm strips.

6 Bring the soup to the boil.

7 Serve the noodles in a deep bowl, arrange the shrimp and spinach on top, and pour in the soup. Garnish with chopped spring onion and *shichimi*.

12

Soba Noodles with Chicken

かしわそば *Kashiwa Soba*

* See page 4 how to cook noodles
* See page 6 how to make noodle soup

Serves 1

100g *soba* noodles
50g chicken thigh
¼ spring onion
350ml noodle soup
some *shichimi*
(optional)

1 Cut the chicken into bite size pieces.

2 Boil up the chicken and soup and cook until chicken is tender, skimming off any scum that forms during cooking.

3 Place the cooked noodles in a deep bowl and pour the soup and chicken over. Garnish with chopped spring onion and *shichimi*.

14

Udon Noodles with Thin Fried Bean Curd

● きつねうどん *Kitsune Udon* ●

Serves 1

100g *udon* noodles

20g fried bean curd
(1 block)

350ml noodle soup

¼ spring onion

some *shichimi*
(optional)

[A]

100ml soup stock

½ tbsp soy sauce

1 tbsp sugar

* See page 5 how to cook noodles
* See page 6 how to make noodle soup

1 Boil the fried bean curd in water for 5 minutes, and then drain. Add A and cook until the sauce is reduced to a third.

2 Bring the soup to the boil.

3 Put the noodles in a deep bowl and lay the bean curd on top, pour over the soup, and sprinkle with chopped spring onion and *shichimi*.

Clay Pot Udon Noodles

鍋焼きうどん *Nabeyaki Udon*

* See page 5 how to cook noodles
* See page 6 how to make noodle soup

Serves 1

100g *udon* noodles

1 shrimp

1 *shiitake* mushroom, stem removed

2 slices *kamaboko*

1 egg

100g spinach

¼ leek

350ml noodle soup

some *shichimi* (optional)

[batter for shrimp tempura]

50g plain flour, sifted

½ egg

some cold water

some vegetable or sunflower oil

1 Make shrimp *tempura* (instructions page 10).

2 Cook the spinach, drain it, and cut it into 5cm lengths. Slice the leek diagonally, 3cm width.

3 Boil the soup and *shiitake* in an individual clay pot. Remove the *shiitake* and add the boiled *udon* noodles. Arrange the shrimp *tempura*, spinach, leek, *shiitake* and slices of *kamaboko* on the top and break the egg over them, cover with the lid and cook again. When the egg is half cooked, remove the pot from the heat. Add *shichimi* to taste.

Udon noodles with Curry Sauce

● カレーうどん *Karē Udon* ●

The unusual combination of Indian curry and Japanese soup stock make this a really exciting and appetising dish.

* See page 5 how to cook noodles
* See page 6 how to make noodle soup

Serves 1

100g *udon* noodles

50g lean pork

¼ onion

¼ spring onion

350ml noodle soup

some *shichimi* (optional)

1. Slice the pork into strips, 2cm width. Cut the onion into 5mm thick slices.

[A]
25g curry paste
1 tsp curry powder

2 Boil the noodle soup, add the pork and onion and cook on a medium heat.

3 Remove 240ml of soup from the pan and mix with A. Stir well with a whisk.

4 Pour the mixture back into the pan and cook it on a medium heat, stirring as it thickens.

Tip!

Mix the curry paste
and powder into the
soup gently so that
they dissolve easily.

5 Finely chop the spring onion,
2mm width.

6

Place the boiled *udon* noodles
in a deep bowl, pour the soup
over and sprinkle with the
spring onion. Add *shichimi*
to taste.

Udon noodles with Miso Soup

味噌煮込みうどん *Miso Nikomi Udon*

Serves 1

100g *udon* noodles
50g chicken thigh
½ leek
1 *shiitake* mushroom
1 egg
25g red *miso* paste
350ml noodle soup
½ tbsp *sake*

* See page 5 how to cook noodles
* See page 6 how to make noodle soup

1 Boil the soup in an individual clay pot then add the boiled noodles and cook for 5-6 minutes.

2 Cut the chicken into bite size pieces. Cut the leek diagonally, 1cm thick. Stem the *shiitake*.

3 Dissolve the *miso* paste into the soup and add the *sake*, chicken, *shiitake* and the leek, cover with a lid, bring to the boil and break the egg over the ingredients. Cover with the lid until the egg is half cooked and it's then ready to serve.

Fried Udon

焼きうどん *Yaki Udon*

Serves 1

100g *udon* noodles

50g lean pork

50g cabbage

½ carrot

½ leek

½ tbsp vegetable or sunflower oil

5g *katsuobushi* (optional)

[A]

½ tbsp soy sauce

1 tsp *sake*

some salt and pepper

* See page 5 how to cook noodles

1 Drain the boiled noodles well. Cut the pork into 1cm cubes. Cut the cabbage into strips, 2cm width, the carrot into fine strips, 2mm x 5cm, and slice the leek diagonally, 5mm.

2 Heat the oil in a frying pan and fry the pork and vegetables. When cooked add the noodles.

3 Add A to season. Serve on a plate and garnish with *katsuobushi*.

26

Chilled Somen Noodles

素麺 *Sōmen*

* See page 5 how to cook noodles
* See page 7 how to make cold soup

Serves 1

100g *somen* noodles

1 *myoga*

¼ spring onion

small piece fresh ginger

2 *shiso* leaves

1 tbsp toasted white
sesame seeds

150ml cold soup

some ice

1　Cut the *myoga* in half lengthways, and cut each half into fine slices, 2mm, soak them in water and drain. Slice up the spring onion and *shiso* leaves, 2mm. Skin and grate the ginger.

2　Drain the boiled *somen* noodles and rinse under running water, squeeze and turn them until the stickiness is removed. Drain the noodles, and arrange them in a bowl with some ice.

3　Serve the cold soup in a deep pot. Arrange the *myoga*, spring onion, ginger, *shiso* leaves, and the toasted sesame seeds on a small plate, these are added to the cold soup depending on taste - before dipping the noodles in.

Chinese Egg Noodle Soup

● ラーメン *Rāmen* ●

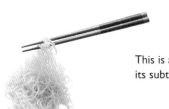

This is a big favourite in Japan and its secret lies in its subtle soy flavour.

Serves 1

100g *ramen* noodles

2 litres water

3 chicken thighs (with bone)

¼ spring onion

* See page 5 how to cook noodles

1 Cook the chicken thighs in boiling water, then drain and rinse.

. . . .

[A]
½ onion
whole celery leaves
vegetable scraps such as
carrot ends, ginger skin,
green leaf vegetables

[B]
5 niboshi
20g katsuobushi

[C]
½ tbsp lard
½ tbsp vegetable oil
1 tbsp soy sauce
1 tsp salt
some pepper

[D]
1 slice roast pork
1 sheet dried seaweed
(21cm x 19cm)
some menma

2 Place the chicken in a deep pan of fresh water, add A, stir and cook on high.

3 Lower the heat just before it's boiled, and remove any scum from the surface. Cook for 1 hour, occasionally skimming off the scum. Once cooked, strain the stock through a colander.

4 Put approx. 1 litre of the stock into another pan, add B and simmer on low heat. Strain it again.

31

. . . .

Tip!

Be careful to wash the chicken thoroughly with running water.

5 Place C in a deep bowl and pour in the stock.

6 Add the boiled noodles to the bowl.

7 Arrange D on the top and garnish with finely chopped spring onion.

Chilled Chinese Egg Noodles

● 冷やし中華 *Hiyashi Chūka* ●

The sour seasoning is great for encouraging the appetite.

Serves 1

100g *ramen* noodles
1 chicken breast
¼ cucumber
2 slices ham
1 egg
some mustard

* See page 5 how to cook noodles

1 Boil the chicken breast, retain the water, and break the meat up by hand.

· ·

[A for the sauce]

1 tbsp water
used to boil chicken

½ tbsp juice
grated ginger

1 ½ tbsp soy sauce

1 ½ tbsp Japanese
vinegar

1 tsp sugar

1 tsp sesame oil

[B]

½ tbsp sesame oil

½ tbsp soy sauce

2 Cut the cucumber 4cm x 2mm, and finely slice the ham, 3mm.

3 Add some salt to the egg and beat, pour a small amount into a heated, lightly oiled frying pan to make a thin sheet of omelette. Make a few sheets, roll them on a chopping board and cut into very fine strips 3mm.

4 Place A in a bowl and mix well.

Tip!

Mix the noodles,
seame oil and soy
sauce by hand, so that
they are thoroughly
coated.

5 As soon as the noodles have
boiled, soak them in cold
water and rinse them well,
turning them under running
water to remove stickiness.
Drain the noodles.

6 Mix B with the noodles well.

Serve the noodles on a plate
and arrange the topping. Add
the sauce and garnish with
mustard.

Chinese Fried Noodles

焼そば *Yakisoba*

Serves 1

100g *ramen* noodles

50g lean pork

50g cabbage

25g carrot

2 tbsp vegetable or sunflower oil

some dried seaweed flakes

some red pickled ginger

[A]

2 tbsp Worcestershire sauce

some salt and pepper

* See page 5 how to cook noodles

1 Cut the pork into strips, 1cm. Chop the cabbage into strips, 2cm, and the carrot 5mm × 2mm.

2 Heat half the oil in a frying pan and fry the pork, cabbage and carrot on a medium heat. When cooked, add the rest of the oil, add the cooked noodles, mix well, and continue frying.

3 Add A and mix well. Serve on a plate, and garnish with dried seaweed flakes and red pickled ginger.

Vegetable Stir-fried Noodles

五目焼そば *Gomoku Yakisoba*

Healthy stir-fried noodle dish with lots of green vegetables.

Serves 1

100g ramen noodles

50g small shrimps

25g bamboo shoot (boiled)

15g carrot

½ pak choi

3g *kikurage*

* See page 5 how to cook noodles
* See page 6 how to make noodle soup

1 Wash the *kikurage*, soak in water for 20 minutes and cut it up, 3cm × 3cm. Slice the bamboo shoot finely, 3mm. Cut the carrot in half lengthways, and then slice each half, 3mm width. Divide the pak choi, cut the leaves into 5cm lengths, and cut the stalk in half lengthways.

Gomoku Yakisoba

1 tbsp vegetable or
sunflower oil

10g cornflour mixed
with 15ml water

½ tsp sesame oil

[A]

350ml soup stock

½ tbsp sake

½ tsp salt

some pepper

2 Heat half the oil in a frying pan, and fry the noodles on a medium heat. When they have browned slightly, take them out and serve them on a plate.

3 Heat the rest of the oil in another frying pan and fry the deveined shrimps.

4 When the shrimps are cooked, turn up the heat and add the *kikurage*, bamboo shoots, carrot, and pak choi and stir-fry them.

Tip!

Stir-fry the vegetables quicky to benefit from the highest vitamin content.

5   Add A to the pan and let it simmer.

6   Add the cornflour (mixed with water) to thicken, and then add the sesame oil.

7   Pour the cooked shrimps and vegetables over the noodles.

Pasta with Salted Cod Roe

たらこパスタ *Tarako Pasta*

Serves 1

100g spaghetti
35g *tarako*
1 clove garlic
some dried seaweed

[A]
10g butter
1/2 tbsp olive oil
some lemon juice

1 Cut the skin of *tarako* with a knife and scoop out the cod roe. Grate the garlic.

2

Place the *tarako*, garlic with A in a bowl and mix well.

3 Mix the ingredients with the cooked spaghetti and a tablespoon of the water it was cooked in. Serve on a plate and garnish with fine strips of dried seaweed.

Japanese Style Pasta

和風パスタ *Wafū Pasta*

Serves 1

100g spaghetti
50g *enoki* mushrooms
50g *shimeji* mushrooms
3 *shiitake* mushrooms
1 tbsp white wine
1 tbsp olive oil
1 tsp soy sauce
some salt and pepper
1 tsp butter
some chives

1 Stem all the mushrooms and finely slice the *shiitake*, 3mm.

2 Heat the olive oil in a frying pan, add the mushrooms, and cook slowly on a low heat. When softened, add the white wine, salt and pepper.

3

Add the cooked spaghetti to the pan and stir-fry it. Once the ingredients are mixed well, add the soy sauce, swirl it around and then add the butter. Serve it on a plate and garnish with chopped chives.

• Guide to ingredients - Noodles •

Abura-age	—	fried bean curd – 1 block refers to 20g (fried tofu)
Aonori	—	dried seaweed flakes
Benishoga	—	red pickled ginger
Dashi	—	Japanese soup stock
Enoki	—	very thin white mushrooms
Kamaboko	—	Japanese fishcake
Katsuobushi	—	bonito flakes
Kikurage	—	Jew's ear
Menma or Shinachiku	—	pickled bamboo shoots
Mirin	—	cooking sake (sweet)
Miso	—	fermented soya bean paste
Myoga	—	Japanese ginger
Niboshi	—	dried sardine
Nori	—	sheet of dried seaweed – 'standard size' refers to sheet: 21cm × 19 cm
Osu	—	Japanese vinegar
Sake	—	Japanese rice wine
Shiitake	—	variety of mushroom
Shichimi	—	seven spice pepper
Shimeji	—	small brown-topped mushrooms
Shiso	—	beefsteak plant
Tarako	—	salted cod roe